To the Occupational Therapy community who gave me the opportunity to work with children everyday.

Let's Play and Learn!

Visit www.thiskidsfuture.com to get exclusive access to super fun play activities that promote toileting hygiene and independence. You will have free access to:

- Peanut Butter Balloons Activities
- Hand Strength & Coordination Activities
- Trunk Range of Motion Activities
- A list of Adaptive Equipment for wiping
- And much more...

I went to Grandma's house,
she made me a PB&J.

I chew, chew, chewed,
and then opened my mouth to say...

"I can use the toilet! I can do it on my own!
If I show you what a big kid I am,
will you get me an ice cream cone?"

Grandma smiled big. She asked, "Well, do you know how to wipe?"
"Yes!" I said to Grandma. "I will show you tonight!"

I brought Grandma to the bathroom. I sat on the toilet seat. "Now I make sure I'm over the bowl," I said. "I'm careful to be neat!"

I hear the plop, plop, plops as I take a glance at the toilet paper.
I may not need it yet, but I will need it later.

When it's time to wipe, I tell Grandma what I've learned,
That I have to do a good job or else I will spread germs.

I also might be stinky if I let poop linger on my bum.
I'd be itchy and feel funny—that would not be much fun!

As I stay seated on the toilet seat,
I grab 4 pieces of toilet paper to fold nice and neat.

As the smell lingers,
I place the folded toilet paper flat on my fingers.

As I start to get in place,
I wipe my butt, and wipe once more,
just in case!

I always wipe front to back, so I don't get ouchies!
Because when I feel uncomfortable, I end up pretty grouchy.

I check the toilet paper, I look to see if there is poop.
If there is, I fold the paper and take another swoop.

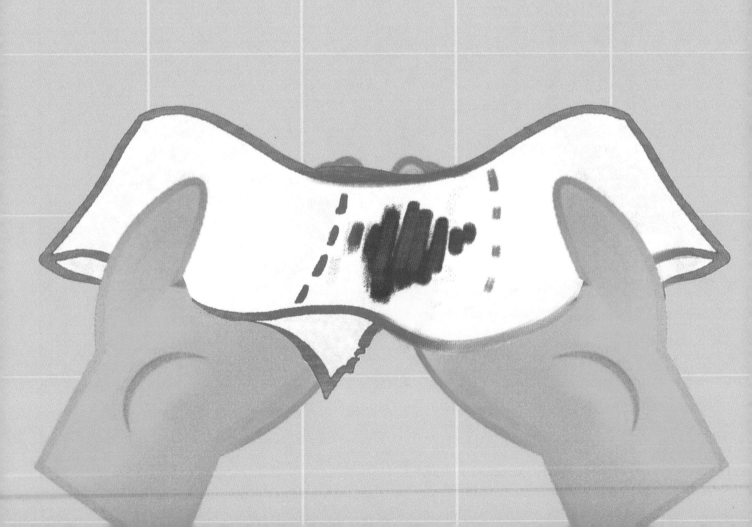

I make sure, as I wipe, to not let poop touch my hands,
Not to let any get on my underwear or inside my pants.

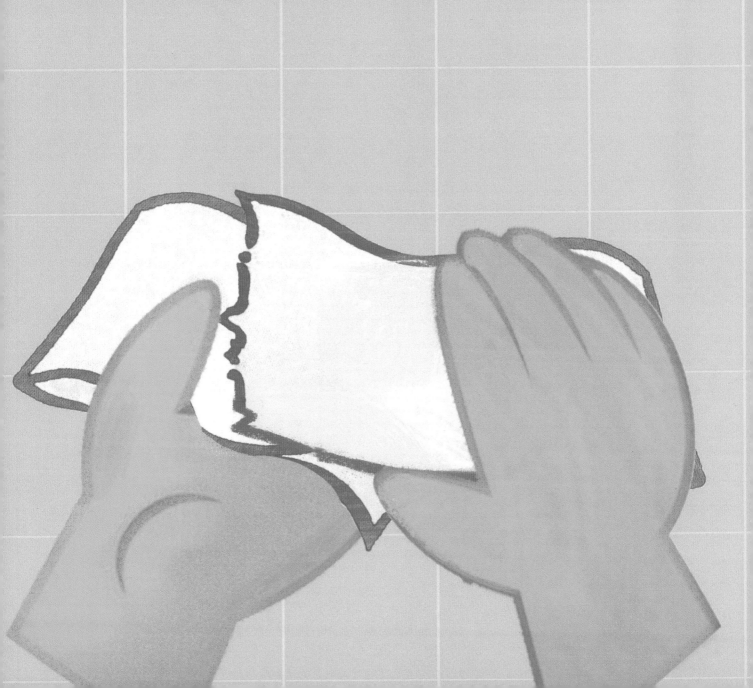

Sometimes when I'm wiping,
it feels like I'm reaching into space.
Even though I can't see there,
I make sure to leave no poop trace.

As I check the toilet paper, I still see a bit of poop,
So I know it's time to wipe again, to give it another scoop.

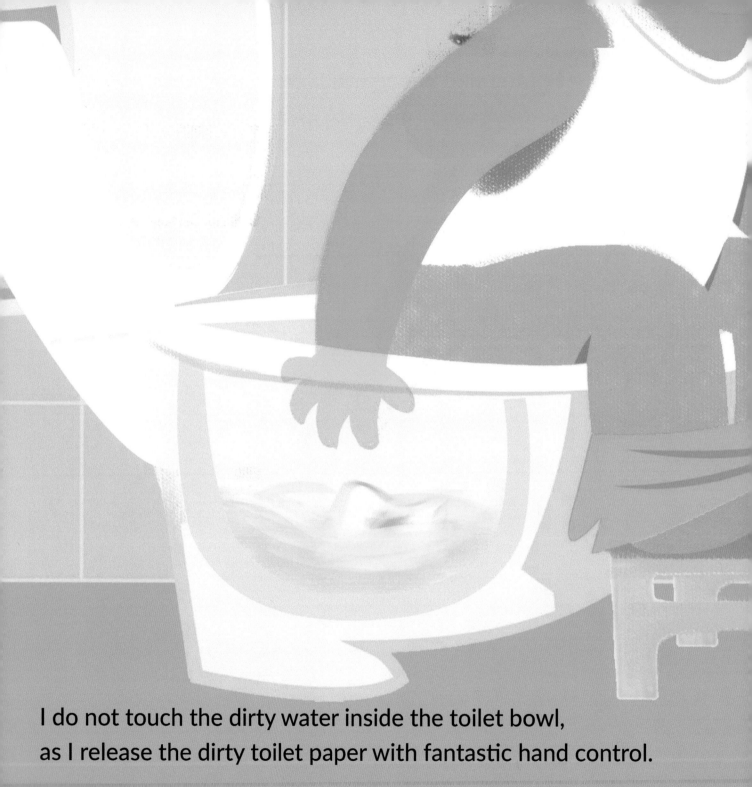

I do not touch the dirty water inside the toilet bowl,
as I release the dirty toilet paper with fantastic hand control.

I know I must keep wiping until the paper is just white,
But I don't mind wiping again, I know that it's alright.

As I check the toilet paper again, I see it's clean and bare.
There's no more poop leftover, no more poop anywhere!

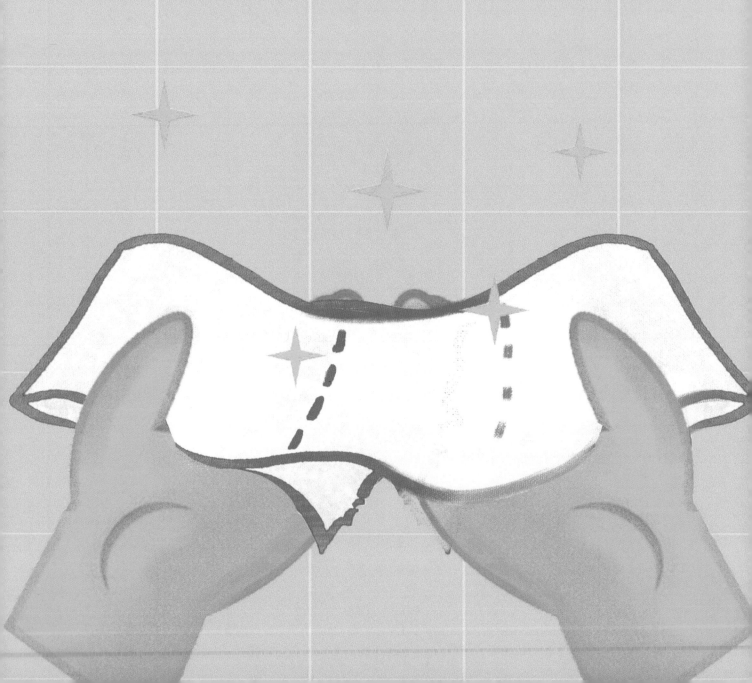

"I'm done! I'm done!" I tell Grandma as I begin to stand,
It's almost time to finish up, to go and wash my hands.

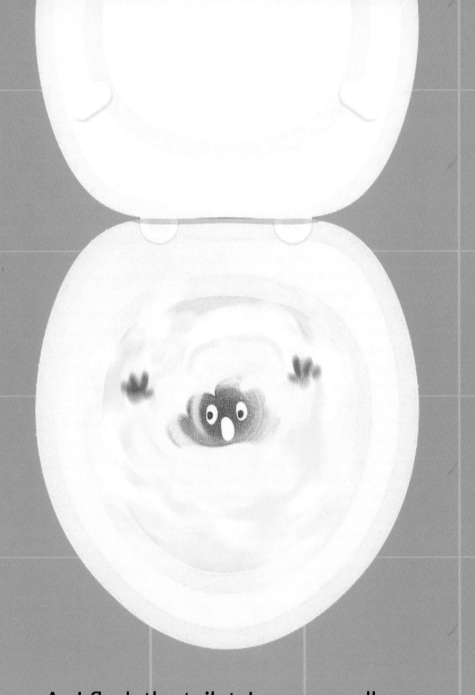

As I flush the toilet, I wave goodbye,
And say "hasta la vista!" to all my little poop guys.

I grab the soap and pump, I scrub and sing my A-B-C's
I put the soap between my hands and give a little squeeze.

I scrub for at least 20 seconds, I make sure my hands are extra clean.
I am so proud of myself because I'm so good at this toileting routine!

I reach for a clean towel, I dry my hands all the way.
I'm done using the toilet, it's now time to play!

I walk out feeling proud, I did it! Hip hip hooray!
Now I can keep going with the rest of my awesome day.

"Good job!" Grandma says to me. "Now that you're nice and clean, get your stuff, it's time to go. It's time to get ice cream!"

Take it from me, it's easy, you know what to do.
The next time you feel funny in your tummy
you need to make a poo!

About Ralph & Arianna

Ralph and Arianna are creators of fun evidence-based toilet training books for children, teens, and pediatric therapists such as the children's book "Now I Know, How To Go, Potty!" and "Pediatric Potty Training" for pediatric therapists.

Arianna has worked with many children one on one as a pediatric Occupational Therapy Assistant to help achieve their individualized toileting goals.

Ralph is a visionary whose mission is to promote confidence and positive self-esteem through his books.

Together, they are passionate about promoting independence, participation, and positive relationships for the children and teens going on to shape the future.

Printed in Great Britain
by Amazon

44267859R00018